BRIAN MOORE   ALASDAIR GRAY

JOHN McGAHERN

A BIBLIOGRAPHY OF THEIR FIRST EDITIONS

BRIAN MOORE   ALASDAIR GRAY

JOHN McGAHERN

A BIBLIOGRAPHY OF THEIR FIRST EDITIONS

David Rees

Colophon Press Bibliography Series No.1

Published at The Colophon Press, 18a Prentis Road, London SW16 1QD.

© 1991 David Rees

Numbered edition: ISBN 1 874122 00 8
Lettered edition: ISBN 1 874122 01 6

First published 24 October 1991

This bibliography is published simultaneously with Catalogue 26.

Typeset by Lyndon Green, Enderley Cottage, Selsley East, Stroud, Glos. GL5 5JY.
Printed in England

CONTENTS

INTRODUCTORY NOTE

All measurements have been given in centimetres regardless of which scale they were in fact made in. Pagination includes unnumbered preliminaries in Roman, numbered pages in Arabic, and includes all blank leaves; where there are no endpapers the pasted down leaves have been included. Endpapers are blank unless otherwise stated.

Dates have been given without brackets irrespective of whether they appear on the recto or the verso of the title page.

Proofs have only been included where copies are also included in my simultaneously issued Catalogue 26; it is to be assumed that bound proofs were made in all cases except where stated (see notes to Alasdair Gray A3(a), A4(a) and A6(a)). Proof wrappers are plain unless described as specific publisher's wrappers, which indicates that they are ornamented with the publisher's device. Proof dustwrappers have the same design as published dustwrappers unless described as variant dustwrappers.

I have consulted four previously published bibliographies of Brian Moore: Hallvard Dahlie's in 'Brian Moore', Studies in Canadian Literature series, Toronto, 1969: Jeanne Flood's in 'Brian Moore', Irish Writers Series, Associated University Presses, 1974; Richard Studing's in Irish University Review, vol.18, 1975; and Brian McIlroy's in Irish University Review, Spring 1988. Hallvard Dahlie also compiled the bibliography included in 'The Brian Moore Papers: First Accession and Second Accession', University of Calgary Press 1977, the inventory of Moore's papers lodged at Calgary University Library. I have consulted one previously published bibliography of Alasdair Gray, that in Scottish Book Collector, issue 7, August 1988.

I would like to thank all the institutions and individuals who have helped with the Brian Moore section of this bibliography, in particular: Marlys Chevrefils at Calgary University Library, Jeffrey Pressman, Carl Spadoni at McMaster University Library, Anne McDermid and Grace Wherry at Curtis Brown Ltd., Jonathan Cape Ltd., Reading University Library, Hallvard Dahlie, Richard Williams, Jack Adrian, William Hoffer, Nelson Ball, Steven Temple and Thomas Lesser. I would also like to thank William Cowan and Canongate Publishing Ltd. for help with Alasdair Gray.

David Rees

BRIAN MOORE 'A' ITEMS

I have been unable to ascertain the exact publication dates for the Canadian editions of A15, A18, A19, A21 and A23. Records at Calgary University Library indicate that publication in each of these cases was simultaneous with the American edition. As these editions were made from American sheets, I have however assumed in each case the American edition to be the first edition.

There is some evidence, both at Calgary and at the McClelland and Stewart archives at McMaster University, that the Canadian edition of A14 preceded the American, and I have therefore listed it as being the first edition.

A22 is shown at Calgary as being simultaneous, but McClelland and Stewart state that the American preceded.

None of the proofs listed below has significant textual variations from the published books.

Print-runs and publications dates have been obtained from several sources. The print-runs for the Harlequin, Dell and Deutsch editions, and the publication dates for all the American editions from A13-A22, were extracted from Calgary. These were confirmed by Moore's American agents, Curtis Brown of New York, who also supplied the dates for the American editions of A7, A8, A9, A10, A11 and A23. Curtis Brown gave 15 May 1956 for the American edition of Judith Hearne, Calgary 12 June 1956, and here I have favoured the latter. Print-runs and publication dates for the Cape editions were extracted from Cape's records. Publication dates for the English Gold Medal and Red Seal editions were obtained from the Dragonby Bibliographies, compiled and published by Richard Williams. Months of publication of some of the Canadian editions was confirmed by McMaster University.

A1   WREATH FOR A REDHEAD   1951

(a)   *First edition.* Harlequin Books no.102, Toronto, March 1951. 17.2 x 10.7 cm. Pp: 128. Pictorial wrappers lettered in white and yellow on upper panel; white on spine; red, yellow, black and blue on (white) lower panel. All edges red. Print-run: 19,366.
Royalty slips at Calgary show that 13,988 copies were sold by 30 April 1952.

(b)   *First American edition, published as 'Sailor's Leave' sub-titled (Wreath For A Redhead).* Pyramid Books no.94, New York, 1953. First edition thus. 16.2 x 10.7 cm. 25¢. Pp: 158,ii. Pictorial wrappers lettered in black, red, white and yellow on upper panel; black and red on spine; black and red on (white and yellow) lower panel. All edges blue.

A2   THE EXECUTIONERS   1951

(a)   *First edition.* Harlequin Books no.117, Toronto, June 1951. 17 x 10.5 cm. Pp: 157,iii. Pictorial wrappers lettered in red, white and yellow on upper panel; white and yellow on (red) spine; red, blue and black on (white) lower panel. All edges red. Print-run: 20,322.
Royalty slips at Calgary show that 16,208 copies were sold.
No American edition.

A3   FRENCH FOR MURDER   1954

(a)   *First edition, published under the pseudonym 'Bernard Mara'.* Gold Medal Book no.402, Fawcett Publications, New York, May 1954. 18 x 10.7 cm. 25¢. Pp: 144. Pictorial wrappers lettered in red, yellow and white on upper wrapper; black, red and green on (yellow) spine; black on lower panel.
No separate Canadian edition. The American edition was distributed in Canada with a Canadian price sticker (35¢) over the American price
Upper wrapper states 'An Original Gold Medal Novel/NOT A REPRINT'.

(b)   *First English edition, published under the pseudonym 'Bernard Mara'.* Red Seal no.53, L. Miller & Sons, London, 17 October 1956. 2/-. 159pp. Printed in The Netherlands. Wrappers as A3(a) except for different publisher's device, number and price.

A4   A BULLET FOR MY LADY   1955

(a)   *First edition, published under the pseudonym 'Bernard Mara'.* Gold Medal Book no.472, Fawcett Publications, New York, March 1955. 18 x 10.6 cm. 25¢. Pp: 156,iv. Pictorial wrappers, lettered in black and white on upper wrapper; black and red on (yellow) spine; black on lower panel.
No separate Canadian edition.

(b)   *First English edition, published under the pseudonym 'Bernard Mara'.* Gold Medal Book no.124, Frederick Muller Ltd., London, 26 March 1956. 2/-. Pp: 156,iv. Printed from first-edition plates. As A4(a) except for different number and price on wrappers, extract from the book absent from first preliminary (replaced by half-title), and different copyright information (copyright page states "Printed at the Phillips Park Press, Manchester, and published in Great Britain by Frederick Muller Ltd. by arrangement with Fawcett Publications Inc.").

(a)   *First edition.* Andre Deutsch, London, 17 May 1955. 19 x 12.5 cm. 10s 6d.
       Pp: 223,i. Maroon boards, gold blocked on spine. White endpapers. Light
       brown dustwrapper (white on lower panel) printed in red and black. Print-
       run: 3000.

(b)   *First American edition, as 'The Lonely Passion Of Judith Hearne'*. Little,
       Brown & Company, Boston and Toronto, 12 June 1956.

(c)   *First Canadian edition.* McClelland & Stewart, Toronto, 1964. A New
       Canadian Library paperback.
       Records at Calgary show that an edition was due to be published by William
       Collins & Sons, Toronto, on 20 August 1955; this is listed in Hallvard Dahlie's
       bibliography, published in 1969. I have been unable to find any trace of this edition
       (there is no copy in the National Library of Canada, for example, and Dahlie's in-
       formation was based solely on the records at Calgary); it is almost certain, there-
       fore, that this edition was not in fact published.

(d)   *First American paperback edition, as 'The Lonely Passion Of Judith Hearne'*. Dell
       Publishing Company, New York, September 1957. 16.2 x 10.5 cm. 35¢. Pp:
       256. Yellow wrappers with white snowflakes lettered in red and black. All
       edges blue-green.

A6   THIS GUN FOR GLORIA   1956

(a)   *First edition, published under the pseudonym 'Bernard Mara'*. Gold Medal
       Book no.562, Fawcett Publications, New York, March 1956. 18.2 x 10.8 cm.
       25¢. Pp: 144. White pictorial wrappers (yellow on spine) printed in red,
       yellow, blue and black. All edges yellow.
       No separate Canadian edition.

(b)   *First English edition, published under the pseudonym 'Bernard Mara'*. Gold
       Medal Book no.172, Frederick Muller Ltd., London, 28 February 1957. 2/-.
       Pp: 144. Differs from A6(a) as A4(b).

A7   INTENT TO KILL   1956

(a)   *First edition, published under the pseudonym 'Michael Bryan'*. Dell First
       Edition 88, Dell Publishing Company, New York, 9 February 1956. 16.3 x
       10.8 cm. 25¢. Pp: 191,i. Red pictorial wrappers printed in blue, white,

yellow and black. All edges red. Print-run: 205,000.

16,000 copies were printed with a price of 35¢ for distribution in Canada. The true authorship of the pseudonymous titles was not established until the 1970s; despite their high print-runs, relatively few copies survive.

(b)   *First British edition, published under the pseudonym 'Michael Bryan'.* Eyre & Spottiswoode, London 1956. 19 x 12.4 cm. 10s 6d. Pp: 190,ii. Red boards lettered in black on spine. White endpapers. Black dustwrapper (white on lower panel) printed in red, white and black.

Some copies were issued in blue boards.

A8   THE FEAST OF LUPERCAL   1957

(a)   *First edition.* Little, Brown & Company, Boston and Toronto, 28 March 1957. 21 x 14 cm. $3.75. Pp: x,246. Black and yellow boards lettered in black on spine. White endpapers. Green dustwrapper (white on lower panel) printed in black, white and orange.

(b)   *First English edition.* Andre Deutsch, London, 1958. 19 x 12.5 cm. 15s. Pp: 240. Red boards, gold blocked on spine. White endpapers. Green pictorial dustwrapper (white on lower panel). Print-run: 3500.

Re-published by Longacre in 1960 as 'A Moment Of Love'.

A9   MURDER IN MAJORCA   1957

(a)   *First edition, published under the pseudonym 'Michael Bryan'.* Dell First Edition A145, Dell Publishing Company, New York, 20 August 1957. 16.2 x 10.5 cm. 25¢. Pp: 158,ii. Pictorial wrappers (black on lower panel) lettered in white, blue, red and black. All edges green. Print-run: 200,000.

Some copies were printed with a price of 35¢, for distribution in Canada. Royalty slips at Calgary show that 134,957 were sold.

(b)   *First English edition, published under the pseudonym 'Michael Bryan'.* Eyre & Spottiswoode, London 1958. 19 x 12.4 cm. 12s 6d. Pp: 191,i. Black boards, gold blocked on spine. White endpapers. Blue pictorial dustwrapper (white on lower panel) lettered in red, yellow, white and black.

Some copies were issued in cream boards.

A10   THE LUCK OF GINGER COFFEY   1960

(a)   *First edition.* Little, Brown & Company, Boston and Toronto, 4 August 1960.

(b) *First English edition.* Andre Deutsch, London, 1960. 20.4 x 13.2 cm. 15s. Pp: 222,ii. Red Boards, gold blocked on spine. White endpapers. White dust-wrapper printed in pink, orange, black and green. Print-run: 5000.

A11   AN ANSWER FROM LIMBO   1962

(a) *First edition.* Little, Brown & Company, Boston & Toronto, 19 September 1962. 21.5 x 14 cm. $5.00. Pp: viii,322,i. Reddish-brown boards lettered in gold on spine, with publisher's device on upper panel. White endpapers. Brown dustwrapper (white on lower panel) lettered in red, white and black.

(b) *First English edition.* Andre Deutsch, London, 1963. 20.3 x 13.2 cm. 21s. Pp: 319,i. Brown boards, gold blocked on spine. White endpapers. Dark brown dustwrapper (white on lower panel) lettered in white, blue and black.

(c) *First Canadian edition.* PaperJack 1973. Paperback.

A12   CANADA   1963

(a) *First edition.* Time Incorporated, New York, 1963. 28 x 21.5 cm. Pp: 160. Brown and white pictorial boards lettered in black, grey, red and white. Blue, white and black pictorial endpapers. Published without a dustwrapper.
A guide to Canada, co-written with the editors of Life.
Copyright page states "Published simultaneously in Canada".

A13   THE EMPEROR OF ICE CREAM   1965

(a) *First edition.* The Viking Press, New York, 15 September 1965. 20.9 x 13.9 cm. $4.95. Pp: vi,250. Green boards, quarter bound in cream cloth, lettered in green and orange on spine. White endpapers. White dustwrapper (black on spine) printed in orange, green, black and white. Top edge red.

(b) *First Canadian edition.* McClelland & Stewart, Toronto, 25 September 1965. $5.95. First-edition sheets.

(c) *First English edition.* Andre Deutsch, London, 27 January 1966. 20.4 x 13 cm. 21s. Pp: vi,250. Printed from first-edition plates. Green boards, gold blocked on spine. White endpapers. Dustwrapper as A13(a), except for different publisher, and different photograph and text on lower panel.

A14 I AM MARY DUNNE 1968

(a) *First edition.* McClelland & Stewart, Toronto, 1968. American sheets. Binding as A14(b).

(b) *First American edition.* The Viking Press, New York, 19 June 1968. 21 x 13.8 cm. $4.95. Pp: vi,217,i. Purple boards, quarter bound in yellow cloth, lettered in red and black on spine. Yellow endpapers. White dustwrapper with yellow panels lettered in red and black. Top edge yellow.
Possibly simultaneous with A14(a).

(c) *First English edition.* Jonathan Cape, London, 17 October 1968. 19.4 x 12.9 cm. 25s. Pp: 251,i. Pink boards, gold blocked on spine. White endpapers. White dustwrapper printed in red and pink. Top edge black. Print-run: 5000.

(ci) *First English edition.* Uncorrected proof copy. 18.8 x 12.7 cm. Pp: 251,iii. Setting as A14(c). Green Cape wrappers lettered in black.

A15 FERGUS 1970

(a) *First edition.* Holt, Rinehart & Winston, New York, 14 September 1970. 20.9 x 14 cm. $5.95. Pp: xii,228. Orange boards, quarter bound in red cloth, lettered in gold and black on spine. Orange endpapers. White dustwrapper lettered in green, black, white and orange.

(b) *First Canadian edition.* McClelland & Stewart, Toronto, September 1970. $5.95. First-edition sheets. Binding as A15(a).
Simultaneous with A15(a).

(c) *First English edition.* Jonathan Cape, London, 25 March 1971. 20.3 x 13 cm. £1.75. Pp: x,228,ii. Printed from first-edition plates. Purple boards, gold blocked on spine. White endpapers. White dustwrapper printed in black and orange. Top edge blue. Print-run: 4500.

(ci) *First English edition.* Uncorrected proof copy. 19.8 x 12.7 cm. Pp: x,228. Setting as A15(c). Red Cape wrappers with white label on upper wrapper printed in black. White endpapers.

A16   THE REVOLUTION SCRIPT   **1971**

(a)   *First edition.* McClelland & Stewart, Toronto, 9 October 1971. $6.95. Setting as A16(b). Orange boards.

(b)   *First American edition.* Holt, Rinehart & Winston, New York, 15 November 1971. 22.2 x 14 cm. $6.95. Pp: x,261,i. First-edition sheets. Black boards lettered in red and white on spine. Printed grey endpapers. Black dustwrapper printed in white, red and black.

(c)   *First English edition.* Jonathan Cape, London, 20 January 1972. 22.3 x 13.8 cm. Pp: viii,261,iii. Printed from first-edition plates. Red boards, gold blocked on spine. Printed white endpapers. Dustwrapper as A16(a) except for different publisher, title lettered in white on spine, lower panel unprinted and different text on inner flaps. Top edge black. Print-run: 3485.

A17   CATHOLICS   **1972**

(a)   *First edition.* McClelland & Stewart, Toronto 1972. 22 x 14.5 cm. $4.95. Pp: 107,v. Cream boards, gold blocked on spine. Pale green endpapers. White dustwrapper lettered in gold, red and black.

(b)   *First English edition.* Jonathan Cape, London, 2 November 1972. 20.4 x 13 cm. £1.25. Pp: iv,102,vi. Black boards, gold blocked on spine. No endpapers: outer leaves pasted down. Purple dustwrapper lettered in black, white and gold. Top edge orange. Print-run: 4000.
In the English edition the text is divided into three, rather than four, chapters.

(bi)   *First English edition.* Uncorrected proof copy. 19.6 x 12.8 cm. Pp: iv,102,vi. Setting as A17(b). Olive-green Cape wrappers lettered in black. Gold (variant) proof dustwrapper printed in black and white.

(c)   *First American edition.* Holt, Rinehart & Winston, New York, 15 March 1973. 21.6 x 14.1 cm. $4.95. Pp: 107,v. (Pagination varies slightly from A17(a), the first five paragraphs of chapter 4 being transferred to the end of chapter 3). Red boards, gold blocked on spine. White endpapers. Dustwrapper as A17(a) apart from different text and author's photograph, and has reviews on lower panel.
'Catholics' was first published in America in New American Review 15, 1972.

A18   THE GREAT VICTORIAN COLLECTION   1975

(a)   *First edition.* Farrar, Straus & Giroux, New York, 2 June 1975. 20.9 x 13.9
       cm. $7.95. Pp: viii,213,iii. Yellow boards, quarter bound in black cloth, gold
       blocked on spine. Ornamental margin blind stamped on upper panel.
       White endpapers. White dustwrapper with yellow panel, printed in black,
       white, red and orange.

(b)   *First Canadian edition.* McClelland & Stewart, Toronto, 1975. $8.95. First-
       edition sheets. Binding as A18(a).
       Simultaneous with A18(a).

(c)   *First English edition.* Jonathan Cape, London, 16 October 1975. 20.5 x 12.9
       cm. £3.25. Pp: viii,213,iii. Blue boards, gold blocked on spine. LIght brown
       endpapers. Light brown dustwrapper printed in black and white. Top edge
       blue. Print-run: 4000.

A19   THE DOCTOR'S WIFE   1976

(a)   *First edition.* Farrar, Straus & Giroux, New York, 6 October 1976. 21.6 x 14.3
       cm. $8.95. Pp: viii,277,iii. Light grey boards, quarter bound in brown cloth,
       gold blocked on spine. White endpapers. White dustwrapper (orange on
       spine) printed in black, orange, brown, yellow and white.
       Burgess: 99 novels.

(ai)   *First edition.* Uncorrected proof copy. 20.8 x 13.2 cm. Pp: vi,286,iv. Blue
       wrappers lettered in black.

(b)   *First Canadian edition.* McClelland & Stewart, Toronto, 1976. First-edition
       sheets. Binding as A19(a). Dustwrapper as A19(a) except for publisher's
       name and ISBN number, and a slightly darker shade of orange on spine.
       Simultaneous with A19(a).

(c)   *First English edition.* Jonathan Cape, London, 18 November 1976. 20.5 x 13
       cm. £3.50. Pp: viii,277,iii. Printed from first-edition plates. Black boards,
       gold blocked on spine. Cream endpapers. White dustwrapper printed in
       blue, green, brown, black and white. Top edge brown. Print-run: 6000.

(ci)   *First English edition.* Proof copy. 20.9 x 14 cm. Pp: vi,286. Setting as A19(ai).
       Green wrappers lettered in black.

A20   TWO STORIES   1978

(a)   *First edition.* Santa Susana Press, California State University, 1978. 20.4 x
       13 cm. Pp: ii,58,iv. Reddish-brown boards, gold blocked on (brown) spine.
       Brown endpapers. An edition of 300 numbered and 26 lettered copies, each
       signed by the author. Published without a dustwrapper.
       Only edition. Contains the stories 'Preliminary Pages for A Work of Revenge', first
       published in Midstream 7, Winter 1961, and 'Uncle T', first published in Gentle-
       man's Quarterly, November 1960.

A21   THE MANGAN INHERITANCE   1979

(a)   *First edition.* Farrar, Straus & Giroux, New York, 12 September 1979. 21.5
       x 14.3 cm. $10.95. Pp: x,336,vi. Blue boards, lettered in white on spine.
       Light blue endpapers. Light blue dustwrapper (white on lower panel)
       printed in white, grey, yellow and black. Top edge pink.

(b)   *First Canadian edition.* McClelland & Stewart, Toronto, 1979. First-edition
       sheets. Binding as A21(a).
       Simultaneous with A21(a).

(bi)   *First Canadian edition.* Unbound signatures. 21 x 14 cm. First-edition sheets.
       As A21(a) except for publisher's name on title and copyright pages.
       States "First printing 1979" on copyright page.

(c)   *First English edition.* Jonathan Cape, London, 8 November 1979. 20.5 x 13
       cm. Pp: x,336,vi. Light blue boards, gold blocked on spine. Brown end-
       papers. Top edge blue. White dustwrapper printed in green, blue, pink,
       gold and black. Print-run: 6500.

A22   THE TEMPTATION OF EILEEN HUGHES   1981

(a)   *First edition.* Farrar, Straus & Giroux, New York, 30 June 1981.

(ai)   *First edition.* Uncorrected proof copy. 21.1 x 13.7 cm. Pp: viii,186,ii. Proof
       setting. Blue publisher's wrappers lettered in black.

(b)   *First Canadian edition.* McClelland & Stewart, Toronto, 1981. 21.5 x 14.4 cm.
       $14.95. Pp: x,211,iii. First-edition sheets. Orange boards, quarter bound in
       black, lettered in white on spine. White endpapers. Dark green dust-
       wrapper (white on lower panel) lettered in red, white and black.

(c)   *First English edition.* Jonathan Cape, London, 1 October 1981. As A22(b) except for publisher's name and copyright information. Pink dustwrapper lettered in gold, red and black, with a black-and-white photograph of the author on lower panel. Print-run: 4500.

(ci) *First English edition.* Uncorrected proof copy. 20.5 x 14.5 cm. Pp: vi,211,iii. Setting as A22(c). Red Cape wrappers lettered in black.

A23   COLD HEAVEN   1983

(a)   *First edition.* Holt, Rinehart & Winston, New York, 12 August 1983. 23.5 x 15.4 cm. $14.95. Pp: x,265,i. Light blue boards, quarter bound in dark blue cloth, gold blocked on spine. White endpapers. Blue and black dustwrapper lettered in gold and white. Black-and-white photograph of the author on lower panel.

(ai) *First edition.* Uncorrected proof copy. 21.2 x 13.8 cm. Pp: xii,246,vi. Proof setting. Orange publisher's wrappers lettered in black.

(b)   *First Canadian edition.* McClelland & Stewart, Toronto, September 1983. $18.95. First-edition sheets. Binding as A23(a).

(c)   *First English edition.* Jonathan Cape, London, 27 October 1983. 22.2 x 14 cm. £7.95. Pp: 271,i. Blue boards, gold blocked on spine. White endpapers. Dustwrapper as A23(a) except for different publisher's name and different photograph of the author on lower panel. Print-run: 5000.

(ci) *First English edition.* Uncorrected proof copy. 20.5 x 13.8 cm. Pp: 263,i. Red Cape wrappers lettered in black. Proof dustwrapper is unlaminated and states PROOF ONLY with provisional publication date on lower flap.

A24   BLACK ROBE   1985

(a)   *First edition.* E.P. Dutton, New York, 27 March 1985. 21.8 x 14.1 cm. $15.95. Pp: x,246. Black boards lettered in red and black on (white) spine. White endpapers. Black dustwrapper printed in red and white.

(b)   *First Canadian edition.* McClelland & Stewart, Toronto, 1985. First-edition sheets. Binding as A24(a).

c) *First English edition.* Jonathan Cape, London, 30 May 1985. 22.2 x 13.8 cm. £8.95. Pp: x,246. Printed from first-edition plates. Black boards, gold blocked on spine. White endpapers. Black dustwrapper printed in blue, white and green. Print-run: 7000.

ci) *First English edition.* Uncorrected proof copy. 21 x 13.6 cm. Pp: xii,241,iii. Setting as first-edition proof. Red Cape wrappers printed in black. Black (variant) proof dustwrapper printed in grey, white, green and brown; states PROOF ONLY and gives provisional publication date on lower flap; unlaminated.

cii) *First English edition.* Unbound signatures. 21.6 x 13.8 cm. As A24(c).

d) *Limited edition.* Jonathan Cape sheets bound by the booksellers Kenny's of Galway in an edition of 50 numbered copies, each signed by the author. 22.3 x 14 cm. Pagination as A24(c). Marbled paper over boards, red leather quarter binding with five raised bands tooled in gold, title and author gold blocked on a black label inserted between the top and second band. Grey endpapers, with an extra leaf. No dustwrapper. Blue and white cardboard slipcase.

A25   THE COLOR OF BLOOD   1987

a) *First edition.* E.P. Dutton, New York, 14 September 1987. 21.6 x 14 cm. $16.95. Pp: x,182. Black boards, silver blocked on spine. Red endpapers. Black dustwrapper printed in red, yellow, blue and white.

b) *First Canadian edition.* McClelland & Stewart, Toronto, 1987. First-edition sheets.

c) *First English edition, as 'The Colour Of Blood'.* Jonathan Cape, London, 24 September 1987. 22.2 x 14 cm. £10.95. Pp: viii,182,ii. Printed from first-edition plates (i.e. with the word "colour" spelt "color" in the text). Maroon boards gold blocked on spine. White endpapers. Black dust-wrapper printed in white, blue, red and yellow.

ci) *First English edition, as 'The Colour Of Blood'.* Uncorrected proof copy. 20.4 x 13.7 cm. Pp: 204. Setting as first-edition proof. Red Cape wrappers printed in black.

(a)   *First edition.* Bloomsbury Publishing, London, 19 April 1990. 24.2 x 16 cm.
        £12.99. Pp: viii,194,vi. Blue boards, gold blocked on spine and upper panel.
        Blue endpapers with publisher's device. Blue, white and light brown dust-
        wrapper printed in black, white and gold. Print-run: 20,000.

(ai)   *First edition.* Uncorrected proof copy. 23.4 x 15.3 cm. Pp: viii,194,ii. Setting
        as A26(a). Light blue and white Bloomsbury wrappers printed in dark
        blue, with a photograph of the author on upper panel. Proof dustwrapper
        dark grey (rather than light brown) on upper panel, unlaminated and
        slightly larger than published dustwrapper.

(aii)   *First edition.* Uncorrected proof copy. As A26(ai). Blue and white (variant)
        proof dustwrapper printed in black, white, red and orange, unlaminated,
        and with different photograph of author and slightly different text on
        flaps.

(b)   *Limited edition.* Bloomsbury sheets bound by London Limited Editions in
        an edition of 250 numbered copies, each signed by the author. 24 x 16 cm.
        £32. Pp: xvi,194,vi. Marbled paper over boards, black cloth quarter binding
        gold blocked on spine. No endpapers (outer leaves pasted down). Plain
        light glassine dustwrapper.

(c)   *First Canadian edition.* McClelland & Stewart, Toronto, 1990.

(d)   *First American edition.* Doubleday, New York, September 1990. 24.2 x 15.9
        cm. $18.95. Pp: x,197,i. Orange boards, quarter bound in black, gold
        blocked on spine. Grey endpapers. Grey dustwrapper printed in black,
        white, red and orange.

ALASDAIR GRAY 'A' ITEMS

All the proofs listed below have proof settings, except where stated, although no significant textual differences were found.
Cover design and illustrations are in all cases by the author.
Print-runs and publication dates have been extracted from the publishers' records.

A1   DIALOGUE   1971

(a)   *First edition.* Scottish Theatre Magazine, 1971. Play. 26pp. White(?) wrappers. Published in the 'Play Of The Month' series.
Originally broadcast by the BBC as a radio play in 1969, subsequently as a television play in 1972.
No other edition.

A2   THE COMEDY OF THE WHITE DOG   1979

(a)   *First edition.* Glasgow Print Studio Press, Glasgow 1979. 24.8 x 19 cm. 24pp. 600 numbered copies in wrappers, priced at 75p, with an additional 26 signed lettered copies at £1.75. White card wrappers printed in black.
200 copies were returned to the author in 1984 and subsequently destroyed.
No other edition, although the first half of 'The Comedy Of The White Dog' appeared in Scottish International Magazine 1969, the whole in Glasgow University Magazine 1970, and subsequently in 'Unlikely Stories Mostly' (1983).

A3   LANARK   1981

(a)   *First edition.* Canongate Publishing, Edinburgh, 26 February 1981. 24.2 x 15.9 cm. £7.95. Pp: x,560,vi. American sheets. Black boards, gold blocked on spine. Red endpapers. White dustwrapper printed in black and green. Print-run: 3000.
Burgess: 99 novels.
There were no bound proofs of this edition.

(b)   *First American edition.* Harper & Row, New York, 1981. First-edition sheets.
Published simultaneously with A3(a).

(c)   *Second, limited, edition.* Canongate Publishing, Edinburgh, 1985. 24.1 x 15.8 cm. £15. Pp: viii,560,viii. Setting as A3(a). Black boards, gold blocked on spine and panels. Red endpapers. Light brown dustwrapper printed in black, white and green. An edition of 1000 copies, each numbered, signed and dated by the author on the free front endpaper.

A4   UNLIKELY STORIES MOSTLY   1983

(a)   *First edition.* Canongate Publishing, Edinburgh, 17 February 1983. 19.2 x 12.7 cm. £7.50. Pp: xii,271,v. Blue boards, gold blocked on spine and panels. Decorated white endpapers. White dustwrapper printed in black, red and green. Print-run: 3000.

Published with a mock erratum slip which reads: ERRATUM/This slip has been inserted/by mistake.
There were no bound proofs of this edition.

A5   1982, JANINE   1984

(a)   *First edition.* Jonathan Cape, London, 26 April 1984. 22.3 x 14 cm. £8.95 (later £9.95). Pp: ii,345,iii. Black boards, gold blocked on spine and panels. Red endpapers. White dustwrapper printed in black and red. Print-run: 6000.

Later first edition copies were priceclipped and re-issued at £9.95.

(ai)   *First edition.* Uncorrected proof copy. 20.7 x 13.9 cm. Pp: 347,i. White pictorial wrappers printed in red and black. Proof dustwrapper is slightly larger than the published dustwrapper, and states PROOF ONLY, with provisional publication date, on lower flap.

Dustwrapper design is reproduced on the proof wrappers.

A6   THE FALL OF KELVIN WALKER   1985

(a)   *First edition.* Canongate Publishing, Edinburgh, 1985. 20.5 x 13.2 cm. £7.95. Pp: viii,144. Grey boards, silver blocked on spine and panels. Blue endpapers. White dustwrapper printed in black and blue. Print-run: 3850.

An additional 400 sets of sheets were printed for James Askew.
There were no bound proofs of this edition.

A7   5 SCOTTISH ARTISTS RETROSPECTIVE SHOW   1986

(a)   *First edition.* Famedram Publishers, Gartocharn, November 1986. 5 Colour Catalogues and an Introduction. Six separate items, each 29.3 x 21.2 cm. The introduction consists of eight unnumbered stapled pages; each catalogue is a single leaf, folding out to make six consecutive illustrated pages, and is blank on reverse.

Catalogue for an exhibition organized by Gray. The featured artists were Gray himself, Alasdair Taylor, Carole Gibbons, John Connolly and Alan Fletcher.

A8   ALASDAIR GRAY   1988

a)   *First edition.* The Saltire Society, Edinburgh, 1988. Saltire Self-Portrait no.4.
      18.5 x 11.5 cm. £2. Pp: iv,19,i. Blue pictorial wrappers printed in black and
      white; verso of wrappers white printed in black. No dustwrapper. Print-
      run: 2000.
      No other edition.

A9   OLD NEGATIVES   1989

a)   *First edition.* Jonathan Cape, London, 23 March 1989. Four Verse
      Sequences. 23.5 x 13 cm. £15. Pp: 67,i. Black boards, silver blocked on
      spine and panels. White endpapers. White dustwrapper printed in black.
      An edition of 500 copies, each numbered, signed and dated by the author
      on the free front endpaper.
      Published with an erratum sheet reproducing Gray's manuscript containing a
      lengthy list of alterations he wishes the reader to "correct for him".

ai)   *First edition.* Uncorrected proof copy. 20.3 x 12.9 cm. Pp: 67,i. Red Cape
      wrappers printed in black.

A10   McGROTTY AND LUDMILLA   1990

a)   *First edition.* Dog and Bone Press, Glasgow, 1990. 19.7 x 12.9 cm. £5. Pp:
      132,xii. Blue paper wrappers printed in white, blue and gold. No end-
      papers. No dustwrapper. Print-run: 3000.
      'McGrotty & Ludmilla or The Harbinger Report' was originally conceived as a
      television play, but was first produced as a radio play, broadcast by the BBC on
      18 July 1975. A stage version, 'The Harbinger Report', was subsequently per-
      formed at the Tron Theatre, Glasgow, in February 1987.

A11   SOMETHING LEATHER   1990

a)   *First edition.* Jonathan Cape, London, 12 July 1990. 22.3 x 14 cm. £12.95. Pp:
      251,v. Blue boards, gold blocked on spine and panels. Yellow endpapers.
      White dustwrapper printed in black and red.

ai)   *First edition.* Uncorrected proof copy. 21.2 x 13.8 cm. Pp: x,249,i. Red
      pictorial wrappers printed in black, white and grey.
      Dustwrapper design is reproduced on the proof wrappers.

JOHN McGAHERN 'A' ITEMS

Faber have been unable to supply exact publication dates or print-run figures, but claim total hardback sales (i.e. including reprints) of 50,000 for 'Amongst Women'.

A1   THE BARRACKS   1963

(a)   *First edition.* Faber and Faber, London, 1963. 19 x 12.4 cm. Pp: 232. Red boards, gold blocked on spine. White endpapers. Black dustwrapper (white on lower panel) lettered in black, green and white.

A2   THE DARK   1965

(a)   *First edition.* Faber and Faber, London, 1965. 19 x 12.4 cm. 21s. Pp: 191,i. Black boards lettered in white on spine. White endpapers. Grey-blue dustwrapper (white on lower panel) lettered in dark blue and black.

A3   NIGHTLINES   1970

(a)   *First edition.* Faber and Faber, London, 1970. Short stories. 20.7 x 13.5 cm. 30s/£1.50. Blue boards, gold blocked on spine (with the title on a black panel bordered in gold). White endpapers. Grey-blue dustwrapper (white on lower panel) lettered in black, white and grey.

A4   THE LEAVETAKING   1974

(a)   *First edition.* Faber and Faber, London, 1974. 20.4 x 13 cm. £2.50. Pp: vi,195,vii. Black boards, silver blocked on spine. No endpapers (outer leaves pasted down). Grey-blue dustwrapper printed in black and white.

A5   GETTING THROUGH   1978

(a)   *First edition.* Faber and Faber, London, 1978. Short stories. 20.4 x 13.1 cm. £4.25. Pp: iv,151,v. Blue-grey boards, gold blocked on spine. No endpapers (outer leaves pasted down). Grey-blue dustwrapper (lighter shade on lower panel) printed in black, white and grey.

THE PORNOGRAPHER 1979

a) *First edition.* Faber and Faber, London, 15 November 1979. 20.3 x 13 cm. £4.95. Pp: 252,iv. Light brown boards, gold blocked on spine. Orange-brown dustwrapper printed in black and white.

ii) *First edition.* Uncorrected proof copy. 19.7 x 12.8 cm. Pp: 252,vi. Setting as A6(a). Light blue Faber wrappers lettered in black.

7 HIGH GROUND 1985

a) *First edition.* Faber and Faber, London, 1985. Short stories. 22 x 14 cm. £8.95. Pp: 156,iv. Blue-grey boards, gold blocked on spine. White endpapers. Blue dustwrapper (white on lower panel) printed in black and white.

8 AMONGST WOMEN 1990

a) *First edition.* Faber and Faber, London, 1990. 24.1 x 15.5 cm. £12.99. Pp: vi,184,ii. Orange boards lettered in black on spine. White endpapers. Black dustwrapper printed in green, white and orange.

ii) *First edition.* Uncorrected proof copy. 21 x 13.7 cm. Pp: iv,184. Setting as A8(a). Green Faber wrappers lettered in black.

An edition of 600 numbered copies,
with an additional 26 signed copies
lettered A - Z and bound in orange.
This is